Ringed Giant

The Planet Saturn

by Nancy Loewen   illustrated by Jeff Yesh

PICTURE WINDOW BOOKS
Minneapolis, Minnesota

Thanks to our advisers for their expertise, research, and advice:

Lynne Hillenbrand, Ph.D., Professor of Astronomy
California Institute of Technology

Terry Flaherty, Ph.D., Professor of English
Minnesota State University, Mankato

Editor: Jill Kalz
Designers: Amy Muehlenhardt and Melissa Kes
Page Production: Angela Kilmer
Art Director: Nathan Gassman
Associate Managing Editor: Christianne Jones
The illustrations in this book were created digitally.

Picture Window Books
5115 Excelsior Boulevard
Suite 232
Minneapolis, MN 55416
877-845-8392
www.picturewindowbooks.com

Printed in the United States of America.

 All books published by Picture Window Books
are manufactured with paper containing at least
10 percent post-consumer waste.

Library of Congress Cataloging-in-Publication Data
Loewen, Nancy, 1964-
Ringed giant : the planet Saturn / by Nancy Loewen ; illustrated by Jeff Yesh.
p. cm. — (Amazing science)
Includes index.
ISBN: 978-1-4048-3956-4 (library binding)
ISBN: 978-1-4048-3965-6 (paperback)
1. Saturn (Planet)—Juvenile literature. I. Yesh, Jeff, 1971- ill. II. Title.
QB671.L74 2008
523.46—dc22   2007032895

Table of Contents

All Ears

The man knew he had created something special. It was a device made of magnifying lenses that made faraway objects appear closer. He called it a telescope.

But when the man looked through the telescope, he saw something odd. He didn't know what to think. He saw a planet, but strange shapes stuck out on both sides. They looked like ears!

The year was 1610. The man was an Italian astronomer named Galileo Galilei. He was the first person to view the planet Saturn through a telescope.

Saturn

A Ringed Beauty

In the years that followed, telescopes improved. In 1659, a Dutch astronomer named Christiaan Huygens solved Saturn's mystery. The planet didn't have ears. It had rings!

For many years, people thought Saturn was the only planet in our solar system with rings. Now we know that three other planets (Jupiter, Uranus, and Neptune) also have rings. But Saturn's rings are the brightest and easiest to see.

FUN FACT
Saturn has been known since ancient times. It was named after the Roman god of agriculture, or farming.

Saturn's Place in Space

Of our solar system's eight planets—Mercury, Venus, Earth, Mars, Jupiter, Saturn, Uranus, and Neptune—Saturn is the sixth planet from the sun. Its nearest neighbors are Jupiter and Uranus.

Saturn orbits the sun in an oval-shaped path. On average, it is almost 10 times farther away from the sun than Earth is.

Jupiter

Uranus

Neptune

Saturn

Mercury

Venus

Earth

Mars

FUN FACT
Saturn is the second-largest planet,
after Jupiter. Its diameter is 10 times
bigger than Earth's diameter.

EDITOR'S NOTE
In this illustration, the distances between planets
are not to scale. In reality, the distances between
the outer planets are much greater than the
distances between the inner planets.

9

A Gas Giant

Saturn is one of the gas giant planets. Other gas giants include Jupiter, Uranus, and Neptune. These planets don't have a solid, rocky surface like Earth does. They are made mostly of gas.

Saturn's outer layers are made mostly of a gas called hydrogen. These outer layers push inward, toward the planet's center. The gas is pressed together more and more tightly the nearer it is to the center. The gas gets so tightly pressed that it turns into liquid.

FUN FACT
Even though Saturn is large, it is the least dense of the planets. In a giant pool of water, it would float!

A Windy Planet

Saturn has very strong winds. They can reach speeds greater than 1,000 miles (1,600 kilometers) per hour! The winds blow parallel, or even, to the planet's equator, the imaginary line around a planet's middle. The wide strips of wind are called belts and zones.

Scientists have seen white ovals in Saturn's atmosphere. These ovals are probably hurricane-like storms.

Days and Years

All planets spin, or rotate, on an axis. One complete turn is called a day. A day on Saturn lasts a little less than 11 Earth hours.

A year is the amount of time a planet takes to complete its orbit around the sun. Because Saturn is farther from the sun than Earth is, its year is much longer. A year on Saturn lasts a little more than 29 Earth years.

FUN FACT
Saturn bulges at the middle and is slightly flattened at its north and south poles. This bulging is due to the planet's fast rotation.

15

Rings Around the Planet

Viewed through a telescope, Saturn's rings look solid. But they're not.
They're actually made of billions of pieces of ice and rock. Some of the pieces
are as small as a grain of sand. Others are the size of a house!
The pieces of ice and rock orbit together in thin rings.
These rings then group together to
form larger rings.

FUN FACT

Saturn's rings are thousands of miles wide. But they are only about half a mile (0.8 km) thick. The gaps between the rings are about 2,000 miles (3,200 km) wide.

Many Moons

Rings aren't Saturn's only friends in space. The planet also has at least
56 moons—and probably many more!

Many scientists believe that Saturn's rings are the remains of old moons. The moons may have been shattered by rocks flying through space. Or they may have orbited too close to the planet and been broken apart by Saturn's gravity.

FUN FACT
Saturn's largest moon is called Titan. It's bigger than the planet Mercury. In our solar system, only one other moon is larger: Jupiter's Ganymede.

Studying Saturn

In 1997, scientists from the United States, Europe, and Italy launched the *Cassini-Huygens* spacecraft. It reached Saturn in 2004. The spacecraft remains in orbit there.

New information about Saturn is reaching us all of the time. For example, in 2006, scientists learned of a faint ring that had never been seen before. Who knows what we'll discover next?

FUN FACT
Some U.S. spacecraft have flown safely through Saturn's rings.

Dense, Denser, Densest

What you need:

- a box
- lots of old newspapers

What you do:

1. Loosely crumple up some sheets of newspaper and put them in your box. How many can you fit?

2. Now, empty your box and start over. This time, crumple up the sheets of newspaper tightly. How many sheets does it take to fill your box now?

Density is how much matter or mass fills up space. The more matter you can fit into a limited space, the more dense the space becomes. By crumpling the newspaper sheets tightly, you were able to fit more in the box. You increased the density of the space inside of the box.

Look around your home for other examples of density. Here are a few questions to get you started: What's the difference between cream and whipped cream? Which is denser? If you had a large marshmallow and a brownie of about the same size, which one do you think contains more matter? Which is denser?

Fun Facts

- Saturn is very cold at the top of its atmosphere and very hot deep inside its core. The temperature high at the top of Saturn's clouds is about minus 285 degrees Fahrenheit (minus 176 degrees Celsius). Saturn's core is about 21,150 F (11,742 C).

- Saturn's gravity is similar to Earth's. If you weigh 100 pounds (45 kilograms) on Earth, you would weigh about 110 pounds (49.5 kg) on Saturn.

- Saturn's rings are always parallel to its equator. Since Saturn is tipped on its axis, the rings are tipped, too.

- The Roman god Saturn was the father of Jupiter, the king of the gods. The word *Saturday* comes from Saturn.

Glossary

astronomer—a scientist who studies stars, planets, and other objects in space

atmosphere—the gases that surround a planet

axis—the center on which something spins, or rotates

dense—having a lot of mass packed into a limited space

equator—an imaginary line around the center of a planet, between the north and south poles

gravity—the force that pulls things down toward the surface of a planet

orbit—the path an object takes to travel around a star or planet; also, to travel around a star or planet

solar system—the sun and the bodies that orbit around it; these bodies include planets, dwarf planets, asteroids, and comets

telescope—a device with mirrors or lenses; a telescope makes faraway objects appear closer

To Learn More

More Books to Read

Feinstein, Stephen. *Saturn.* Berkeley Heights, N.J.: MyReportsLinks.com Books, 2005.

Rau, Dana Meachen. *Saturn.* Minneapolis: Compass Point Books, 2003.

Richardson, Adele. *Saturn.* Mankato, Minn.: Capstone Press, 2005.

Simon, Charnan. *Saturn.* Chanhassen, Minn.: Child's World, 2004.

On the Web

FactHound offers a safe, fun way to find Web sites related to topics in this book. All of the sites on FactHound have been researched by our staff.

1. Visit *www.facthound.com*
2. Type in this special code: 1404839569
3. Click on the FETCH IT button.

Your trusty FactHound will fetch the best sites for you!

Index

Look for all of the books in the Amazing Science: Planets series:

Brightest in the Sky: The Planet Venus
Dwarf Planets: Pluto, Charon, Ceres, and Eris
Farthest from the Sun: The Planet Neptune
The Largest Planet: Jupiter
Nearest to the Sun: The Planet Mercury
Our Home Planet: Earth
Ringed Giant: The Planet Saturn
Seeing Red: The Planet Mars
The Sideways Planet: Uranus